The Newly Qualifi

Guid

By Sean Oliver McDonald

Dedication

After a long, hard process of writing this book, I have managed to fulfil one of my ambitions – being published. Okay, in part, this is so I can brag to my friends about how great I must be (in truth, I'm not the most the humble person in the world). However, it's also something that I've wanted to do if just to prove to myself that I can do it all: the writing, the editing, the publishing, the formatting (which I'm in the process of doing whilst I write this and wow, is it difficult). I do however, have some thanks to give and this is the perfect place to do so.

Firstly, I'd like to thank my Mum, who has raised me into the person I am today. She did so with a lot of love despite challenging circumstances (and my rather challenging behaviour through various points of my life). She has always stuck by me and supported me in every way possible, including giving me the confidence to push on with this project. Whilst my sister and I may now only reside in second place in her heart (behind the dog), I do appreciate everything she has done for me and continues to do for me.

Secondly, my step-dad (Martin) deserves a lot of credit. He has pushed me relentlessly to make better use of my free-time, set targets, and try to reach them. I thought the idea of creating a more down-to-earth book on teaching for NQTs was a good idea, but like many ideas it would likely have never gone any further. Through his pushing and support, I have worked hard to make this idea into a reality. Whether this book is helpful or not, at least I have made it and will find out. I have his management and mentoring to thank for that as without it, I'd have seen a lot more episodes of The Simpsons in an evening and never started this idea.

Finally, I have a huge breadth of people, both in my personal and professional life, who have supported me and taught me. They have helped to teach me how to teach others. They have shared their philosophies with me and helped me to learn. There are too many to name but thank you to each of them.

Contents

Introduction

Hi there! How are you? You can't tell me of course, because you're reading a book and I'm probably planning a lesson, doing some marking, or playing with my dog somewhere. I read online that I should try to make a connection with my reader and now that I've aced that part, let's get on with it...

In 1979, Douglas Adams published his infamous book: A Hitchhiker's Guide to the Galaxy. In it, he writes about an intergalactic travel guide and describes the front cover having the phrase "Don't Panic" written across it. I slightly resent that he thought of this first as it would have been the perfect way to start this ever-so-friendly guide.

Don't get me wrong - there isn't actually a reason to panic. I just know that if you are reading this book, there is a 99% chance that you are self-motivated and keen to make a good start to your first year of teaching. In that knowledge, there will be a moment, if it hasn't happened already, where you will think to yourself, "What on Earth do I do now?" That moment when something will go haywire and you'll realise that you are the one who must deal with it.

You will, of course.

You will deal it with it like any other top teacher would. But then you'll probably doubt yourself as I and many others before you have (and perhaps still do). I hope that I can reassure you how normal this is and how you will have likely done the wrong thing. Us passionate teachers tend to doubt ourselves too often.

Incidentally, I write this book as an RQT. I decided to write it now rather than later as I currently have a very real memory of the trials and tribulations of an NQT (or even as a trainee teacher). I remember the endless need to evidence everything you've ever done, whilst simultaneously managing a group of thirty-something children who can frankly, smell your fear. I remember the days when it seems that nothing can go right, and you feel utterly out of your depth. On the other side however, I also remember the moments when you reach a child for the first time. The moments when it all starts to fall into place nicely. The moment when your lesson observation goes really well and your Senior Leadership Team (SLT) get a chance to see how good you are as a teacher. See, it isn't all grim!

I'm also not an expert on teaching – whatever I may think. Given this lack of expertise, I'll aim to share with you my ideas and philosophies of things I have tried and that have gone well. Not brilliantly-complicated pedagogical theories that worked in x and y setting, under the expertise of Dr Whatstheirname and therefore must be great. Sometimes, a practical idea from one teacher to another can be a bit more helpful. I also don't have such a strong knowledge of teaching that I risk overcomplicating this guide; in the same way that sometimes a teacher can pull out every weapon in their arsenal to try to help a child understand something, only for another child to come and explain it to them in a few sentences. Hopefully, this more practical guide will help you on the way to having a successful first year of teaching.

Finally, I also write this to share with you my rather chaotic NQT year. Having left university with an unrelated undergraduate degree, I went through a school-based training year (alongside my PCGE) before I joined a new school alongside five other NQTs. The school was located in an underprivileged setting (contrasting my experience to that date) and was under the fear of the dreaded Ofsted call, which came on my birthday – yay!

Throughout the year though, we supported each other with plenty of help from the rest of the school. I kept in touch with many other NQTs at different schools who also faced a wide range of challenges. In addition, I now work closely with another NQT - who despite being amazingly talented and hard-working - also suffers from the same imposter syndrome that you either have or will likely have at some point.

Just a quick side-note on the Ofsted call aspect: don't be worried about it at all! I expected an army of stone-faced corporate-types with suits and briefcases to march into school, start ticking and crossing a checklist, and then start tearing everything to shreds. In reality, the inspector we had was really nice and knew how to find the best bits of the learning going on. She seemed more supportive than anything and gave us tips on how to get better. It was more like a coaching session for the school than a horrific inspection. I've met other inspectors as well and they are all the same: dedicated to teaching. Using all of their expertise, they choose to spend their time supporting schools and teachers, rather than staying on the front-lines in a classroom. They are still down-to-earth though and keen to help people who are in teaching to do a good job, rather than those who thought teaching was easy as it has lots of holidays.

Anyway, back on topic. Fair warning though, I may get side-tracked a lot!

In this short guide, I hope to offer you the support you deserve. I hope to give you the benefit of the experience I have gathered throughout my NQT year and most of my RQT year. Finally, I want to offer you practical ideas for enhancing your teaching which you can take or leave, depending on your setting. I won't be offended – don't worry! Although I may like to think I'm the greatest teacher in the world, I have to admit that I don't know everything. Wow, it pained me to type that last sentence…

Chapter 1 – Stick to your guns

If - like me - you like to start these types of books but fail to get the end, make sure that you at least make it through this short first chapter. This chapter is all about principles. They're key. In the immortal words of Public Enemy: "If you don't stand for something, you'll fall for anything." Knowing my history of quoting songs, that probably means something entirely different to my interpretation. For me, it means that if you don't have – and stick to – your principles, others will lead you with theirs. Their principles may be fine, of course, but I'd far rather have my own – I know they're great because I thought hard to develop them!

Principles are key in teaching as too often do new ideas or initiatives sweep through with surprisingly little thought given to the impact they'll have on learning. They aren't always bad, but you need to know how to make things work, rather than blindly following ideas. You know your pupils best and as such, you need to be the one applying these to your classroom in the right way.

I'm going to list my principles below and will refer back to them throughout this book due to their importance. As far as I'm concerned, these statements make me as a teacher and they will not be broken without very good reason. In all likelihood, you'll have your own version of these and I hope that you will keep the conviction to stand by them.

Principle I - The kids come first.

This may sound obvious to you as you're a dedicated teacher. After all, if you aren't keen on doing the best for the children in your care, why get into teaching? They're kind of a big part of the job. However, you will find that there are two types of teachers: good and bad.

The good teachers are like you, me, and many more you will have met. We might not know everything, but we care. We will do our best for our children, day-in and day-out. We will make it our mission to learn as much as possible about teaching so that we can do a better job. Let's face it, we aren't doing this job for the wage or the joy of marking or the pleasure of working deep into the evening.

There are however, bad teachers: the ying to our yang; the Vader to our Skywalker; the low-calorie yogurt to our three-layer chocolate cake (sorry, I'm newly vegan and really missing chocolate cake - it's all I can think about). These teachers aren't actually bad, I suppose. They are, however, in teaching for the wrong reasons - and it shows! They saw a reasonable wage for a nice job with funny, cute kids and thought that it seemed like a cushy deal considering the thirteen weeks holiday per year. For these teachers, it's a job. They show up, teach a few lessons, mark the books, and go home. Fair enough, I guess.

We however, care. Probably too much. Let's face it though, some of our children need that extra care. We owe it to each of them to dedicate ourselves to their well-being, happiness, and future.

I'm not saying that we should disregard any hope of a social and personal life for the sake of teaching. You can't. You'll burn out and nobody wants that - it doesn't help. I'll take care of this point later though.

To summarise, as long as you put the pupils at the forefront of your professional mind, you'll do great. They are the reason we chose this profession after all.

Principle II – There is no such thing as a bad kid.

Let me set the scene for you: Sunday morning, mid-January in my first year of teaching and I'm in the changing room of my local gym, fresh out of the shower. A guy (probably about mid-fifties) comes out of the sauna across the room to me. He wanders over to my bench, where he's left his clothes, and opens his locker with a courteous head-nod to me. He puts his leg up on the bench and beneath the towel wrapped around his body, I regrettably catch sight of some dangling personal parts. If you're female, do me a favour and ask any man near you about this person and I guarantee he will be able to tell you about his version of him at his local gym. He's the same type of guy that chats to you at the urinal – weird!

As I look everywhere except the space he occupies, he begins to talk to me as if we're close, personal friends. After a few pleasantries, he asks me what I do for a living. "I teach," I say chirpily, proud of my job and loving life. Well that's it; a red rag to a bull. He launches into the same tirade we have all heard fifty million times:

"Urgh, I don't know how you manage that sort of job anymore. My [insert family relation here]'s kids run riot. You know what the problem is, don't you? The lack of discipline. Back in my day, you didn't mess around for your teacher or he'd have chucked a board rubber at your head. You didn't have bad kids back then. Ridiculous

schools now, they have no power. Kids swear and spit and hit people and all that happens is they don't get a 'Well Done' sticker. Ridiculous!"

We've all heard this rant or some variation on it. I have given up arguing with these people now as they really don't want a debate – their opinion is fact. I tend to now just ignore their comment to ask them a question and distract from the topic.

It does raise an issue however. Many people have a perception that children need tough discipline to make them good and if that age-old method doesn't work, they must just be a bad child. There is rarely any consideration for why the child is struggling with their behaviour and as such, no one considers how to support this child. They are just bad. What can you possibly do with a bad child? I will return to this point later in Chapter 5, where I will offer some practical advice to you.

I'm not saying that the unruly-child-ranters are completely wrong, the fierce teacher of the olden days did keep control of the classroom. I would say though, that this strict teacher didn't manage behaviour through fear of consequences. Inadvertently, this teacher has set up firm, solid boundaries in their classroom and it is this which helps pupils to know where they stand with respect to rules.

Children crave rules and they like them to be enforced, especially in less-privileged settings. A teacher with clear rules and expectations is a teacher they can be safe with.

For example, if you clearly lay out your expectation that pupils will not hit each other and that there will be x, y, and z consequences if they do, pupils can feel safe in the knowledge that they won't be randomly hit mid-lesson. This may seem like it can be assumed but really, it can't be for some of our pupils. Some children come from backgrounds where getting a sibling clipping you around the ear is standard. How can they focus on learning when they are half-expecting one of their peers to walk past and hit them?

On the other side of this, if this rule hasn't been clearly communicated to the class and a child does clip someone around the ear, can you be sure that they are being bad? Maybe that is normal to them and even a sign of endearment if it is what their siblings do at home. Maybe they saw it on a cartoon and didn't know it wasn't funny in real life. Given how obvious it is to us adults that hitting is wrong, we are tempted to view this as being a deliberate act of bad behaviour when in actuality, they may not know! Therefore, setting clear rules helps - everyone knows where they stand.

There are some pupils who will struggle with these rules however. Not because they don't want them; they do. In fact, they struggle because they haven't learnt how to manage themselves or their emotions. If you don't recognise that and help, they never will learn these critical life-skills. Most pupils will learn these behaviour skills at home and throughout their time in school, in the same way that they will learn to do arithmetic calculations by being shown, having it explained, and then getting practice. Some of our pupils will not be taught these skills as we'd hope and over time, as they make mistakes, they will be labelled as a 'bad kid', before eventually starting to live up to the hype.

As a good teacher, you should aim to scaffold the emotional learning of these pupils. I'm not saying don't discipline them where appropriate. I am saying, recognise the why.

Why is that pupil being disruptive? Could the work be too hard?

Why is that pupil so angry? What has caused this? Do they know how to calm themselves down?

If you stick to this principle, you'll make sure that you give every child the chances they deserve and need. There aren't bad kids; not one!

Principle III – Get a life.

I'm really not one of these people who believe that a teacher is only good if they surrender their life outside of the classroom and resign themselves to simply working themselves to the grave. It's not that you don't need to work hard, but that you should find a balance. It's better for everybody involved (pupils included) if you find a balance.

"Of course," your non-teaching friends and family will say. "It's not like you work long hours anyway. You only work from about 8am to 3pm and have every weekend off. On top of that, you have a quarter of a year off." Cue your scowl.

"Pfft," they say. "You don't know what a real job is."

I won't advocate physical violence towards these people in this book but...

In reality, teaching is a very high-powered job. You are always on duty and must plan and mark routinely. On top of that, a good teacher will always go the extra mile for their pupils which takes even more time and effort. However, these next few lines are very important; imagine me saying them slowly and putting a lot of emphasis on each word.

You cannot sustain a bad work/life balance. You will burnout. That isn't good for anyone. Not you. Not your class. Not your school.

Yes, every NQT wants to impress and you will need to work hard but be careful. Take a few early nights. Catch up with your friends. Fire up EA Sport's "FIFA" one evening and moan at how you only lost because your controller's buttons are stiff, and the other player must be cheating somehow. On a more serious note though, you need to look after yourself or you won't survive in this profession. Sorry but it's true.

Principle IV – The little things count.

You may agree with this one or firmly disagree, but for me it is the most important things I have learnt this year. The little things add up and they must be right. Often, when the little things are right, the bigger things fall into place more easily.

Take for instance, a display board. That board is the 'Big Thing'. It has been put up to celebrate your pupils' learning and provide them with challenge and help. We all know the theory behind creating a stimulating classroom environment, so I won't bore you with it.

Now imagine that the display board has an incorrect sum on it. It is a tiny, little thing, but it could lead to big consequences. A pupil may read it and form a misconception based on your board. Worse: you might never notice that it was wrong and as such, not even address the misconception with the class. As a side-note, you can guarantee that some adult will notice it at some point too, be it a governor, member of SLT, or even a visitor to school – how embarrassing!

Consider that the display board starts to get a bit messy as pupils accidently knock things off or the sun starts to bleach the paper. On its own, it's a little thing that happens. As part of a bigger picture though, it gives the impression of an untidy or uncared for classroom, which is the big thing. Especially in underprivileged settings, a neat, well-cared for classroom is an important piece of stability and tranquillity in pupil's lives.

If you look after your classroom, the pupils are more inclined to follow your lead and look after their own work and learning. The little things however, could affect that 'Big Thing' for the worst.

I've used only an example of a display board in this section, but I really think it is something important to consider. Little things really matter. They add up. You wouldn't read this book say, if I hadn't taken the time to watch a very boring video on how to get the margins and text spacing correct. If I hadn't, it would be too untidy. That little thing would ruin the whole guide and potentially stop you from reading it altogether!

I really hope I did the margins and text spacing correctly after saying that...

Principle V – Pupils need to think for themselves.

I firmly believe that most pupils in most schools are far too dependent on adults. Not in the sense that they still need them for simple things, but that they trust adults too much. They don't question what they say anymore, and they don't think critically enough. On a philosophical note, I think this problem is part of the reason that society has large swathes of people who believe everything the TV says. As a teacher, I think it is important to break pupils of this dependency and teach them critical thinking skills, regardless of how hard it is to fit into the curriculum.

This isn't just a philosophical idea by the way. I have worked hard to do this my current class (and last class) and it worked wonders. Pupils who think for themselves are more active in their learning and on the whole, more confident. They seek out new ideas and begin to wonder why. As a bonus, they are also easier to challenge as they develop their own challenges for themselves.

I'll share with you an example from my class this year. Note that I have changed all names in this book to Alice, Ben, Charlie and Dan (in large part because I have never taught children with these names, and these are the names used in a long, forgotten class at university). Anyway, this example is of Alice and Ben who have really done well in a maths lesson. Both are year five pupils and have been looking at fractions and different methods on how to use them.

Towards the end of the lesson, I set them a challenge and they both went to work on it together (good communication is a key aspect in the learning of mathematics). The question was long and complicated and involved multiplying two fractions before adding the answer to another fraction, whose denominator was not a multiple of the denominator of the first fraction. It is a question so complicated that even describing it seems confusing.

They returned to me about five minutes later with an answer. Me, having a degree in mathematics and the arrogance to match, smugly told them they were wrong and sent them away to find their mistake. I tend not to help them as the real learning comes from the cognitive conflict arising as they discuss and try new ideas together. I then carried on with my focus group and thought little more of it.

The lesson finished a few minutes later and I instructed the class to pack away and line up for assembly. As the class followed my instructions, Alice and Ben approached me again and swore blind that they had checked everything, and their answer must be right. Now, I'm starting to sound like a bad teacher here but again, I told them they were wrong. They begged to stay behind through assembly to continue working on the puzzle and, impressed by their determined attitude, agreed, and left them under the supervision of another adult, who was using the time to listen to some pupils read.

I returned from assembly a few minutes later (our school don't require teachers to stay in the hall which gives us a surprisingly useful period of time to take interventions or check books to prepare interventions for after-break) and sure enough, they insisted they were right. At this point, I was thinking that there must be a misconception forming that I need to address. "Explain why then," I asked and sat down at a table like a pupil. Loving their chance to write on my whiteboard, they set about showing me their method and, as a teacher keen to develop their understanding, I asked plenty of open-ended question to determine why they were doing each part, and whether they could explain why using their knowledge of mathematical language.

Then it sunk in – I'd made the mistake!

Making mistakes is something we shy from as teachers - it is almost like we feel academically threatened. Actually, it is a useful tool demonstrated in this example as once they explained all of their thoughts to me (and after I'd thrown in a few red-herrings to really test their knowledge), I had to concede that they were right.

They were delighted!

Not that they'd got the question right, but that they had beaten me and therefore, were the greatest mathematicians of all time. By the end of the day, the whole school knew of their success and I was half expecting them to organise a parade to celebrate themselves. I realised though, they had taken a lot out of that problem. They had had to reason and debate their idea. They had to critically analyse their method and then have the confidence to believe that they were right, and they got a huge confidence boost to know that they could do such tricky tasks.

This event has now led to an atmosphere in the classroom that I am not always right. This really helps as it means that pupils think more for themselves and don't just take my word as gospel. I have to prove things to them as they want to know the why, to see if they agree. Even pupils who can find school tricky, are now trying to catch me out and will look to explain their thinking if they think I am wrong. They may be right but if not, I get a chance to see not just the misconception, but why it formed and how they got confused. We can then discuss it with them critically analysing my explanation. Once they get it, it tends to stick more as they have thought more about it.

This is just one example but I'm sure that you can see that the learning potential here is massive! Pupils who think for themselves will engage more with the learning, compared to a passive learner who is just listening to you drone on and on. For example:

Why do we have relative clauses? If they want to know, they will likely remember it more. They can learn not just how to use them, but when and why. When do they become most effective? Without this questioning and interest, the children (who are in your class) will end up using them randomly and not to good effect.

What would happen if we took the bigger number away from the smaller number? What a brilliant introduction into negative numbers! Well, what do you all think? Have a quick chat together. If the pupils are thinking about the learning, they will pose interesting questions. If this were me and a pupil had asked this in a lesson, I'd now throw the rest of the lesson into my drawer for tomorrow. We could experiment and learn all about negative numbers. The child, who has shown an interest in an aspect of mathematics that for all they know, is beyond the curriculum, will not only learn more now that the lesson is child-led, but they will develop more confidence to ask questions. They thought critically, they asked a good question, then they experimented and found out.

I've gone on a bit of ramble about some good teaching ideas but actually, you don't have to work hard on them. Take the example of the little mistake in the display. Which would be more useful to learning? A perfect display board with correct answers or one with a mistake that pupils could try to search out. They will engage far more with the learning if they are examining it critically. You can then briefly discuss it with the class and ensure that they all spot the mistake and are careful to avoid it. Yes, the rule is that your boards shouldn't have mistakes on them, but some rules can be broken in the name of learning!

Conclusion

To conclude this introductory paragraph, you need to have core values as a teacher which you stick to. You'll probably already have them but might not have realised them for what they are yet. I think if you keep these fresh in your mind, and add to them, your teaching can only improve.

Chapter 2 – Starting the year in style

I have to admit, I failed at this. I failed so bad that if they were to give an award for the worst start to the year; I'd have to be the favourite. I turned it around quickly though and I started this year on fire! It was great! I learnt from my mistakes as all of us must do. But why should you learn from just your own mistakes, when you can learn from mine too?

Firstly, get organised. At some point before the school year begins, set aside two or three days to go into your classroom and get prepared. Have your resources and desk organised into a clear system which you can use comfortably. My colleague – the current NQT I mentioned earlier – labelled and organised everything in her classroom and it really helped her. I teased her for it relentlessly, but truth be told, I was quite jealous. It is actually easier for me to go into her classroom and locate things than it is for me to find stuff in mine. She was probably a tad over-organised but to be fair, it has made her (and my) life a lot easier.

One thing I have found especially useful, is my infamous 'Purple Book'. My teaching assistant set this up for me at the start of the year and it's brilliant. It contains each child's name on the left and multiple pages and rows where I can record important information. I can record homework completion; spelling test results; which letters have been handed back in and signed; pretty much anything! My 'Purple

Book' is my bible of classroom information! You may want an equivalent to help you easily locate and record information.

As an extra note, I'd have your medium-term lesson plans clear in your head. Once you get started, it is easy to lose track of what you want to cover in that first half-term. If your plans are there, you don't need to worry about this aspect of your teaching life.

Secondly, prepare a clear routine with clear standards. These standards should be high and relayed to the pupils at every opportunity. This establishes your rule over the classroom and helps the pupils settle in well. No child likes a scatty classroom. An example of this may be:

8:30 *Pupils line up outside the door. They must be quiet and facing forwards before they* *are let into the class. They enter sensibly, hang their coat up, get out their planner and reading book, and begin a set activity.*

***9:00** Pupils receive their Literacy book and begin to write (or stick in) the lesson's objective. When they are finished, they should put their pencil down and face you. The lesson then begins.*

***10:00** Pupils line up in register order for assembly.*

Etc, etc.

I certainly had the routine when I started but probably not the high standards. I think most NQTs feel the same when they start at a new school; they want to be a nice teacher. I don't know if this is worse for male teachers than female. I always felt that as a six-foot-something male with a naturally mean-looking face at rest, I had to prove that I wasn't some horrible drill-sergeant who revelled in the tears of young children. This was probably all in my head, but it did make me be a bit too soft at the start. I was too lax with rules and had to be told to firm up. You can be a nice teacher and hold pupils to high-standards. In fact, that makes you even nicer as you are doing better for the children – they want rules and routines!

This year, as an RQT, I was better prepared. I had very high-standards from the start and I shared these with the pupils in my first lesson (something I strongly recommend). I stuck to these standards and ensured that pupils knew why I had them. I found that my class settled superbly despite the suggestion that they might not, given the volume of 'disruptive' pupils in it.

You'll have heard this phrase a million times but it's true: It is easier to start tight and loosen up later, than it is to start loose and try to tighten up when it goes wrong.

I say this however, in the knowledge that you'll still start too loose; I haven't met anyone who hasn't. When you realise this however, know that I am smugly chanting "I told you so" in a thoroughly irritating voice.

With regards to the other aspects of getting ready for the start of the year, you may want to use this checklist to help you:

1.   **Get your classroom ready.**

Make sure that you've got all of the displays done and all your resources away in well-labelled drawers. Ensure that you have exercise books ready and something already connected to the interactive whiteboard (computer or laptop). You don't want IT trouble just before your first day.

2.   **Know your pupils.**

Ensure that you have an idea of the pupils coming into your class. The best way to do this is usually to catch their old teacher – or teachers - and sit down with them over a cup of coffee. You will want to know about any SEND needs, behavioural issues, friendship troubles, parental involvement, and anything else of note. I'd also make a note of who your Free School Meals pupils are too - they will likely be a focus for your Pupil Progress Meetings.

I'm not saying that you need to know everything, and it should also be a fresh start for every pupil. Just because they misbehaved for another teacher, it doesn't mean that they won't hit it off with you. I am saying however, that going in blind can be a bit daunting and that if you're like me, you'll want at least some idea of what the class is like and what extra needs you must to be prepared to meet and support.

3.   Know the school.

When I say know the school, I don't mean obvious things like its name and address. You should seek to find out two types of information: important and trivial.

The trivial stuff are the things that really don't matter in the wider scheme of things, but that some people get really hung up on. For example, are there assigned parking spaces or is it first-come, first-served? Do you share mugs for coffee or do you bring your own? How are they washed? Do you need to contribute to the dishwasher duty? You'll pick up on these little things as you go but if you're worried, you could ask another staff member.

The important stuff are the things you need to know off the top of your head and consider daily. What are the school priorities? These are a set of action plans that describe how the school will improve itself this year – you need to know them. You need to know them as you will play in a part in those plans throughout the year. You also need to know them because if visitors come into to school, they will be looking to see if you know them and are contributing to the success of the school's plans.

You also need to know the school's safeguarding policy as a matter of course. Not just who the safeguarding lead is, but where things are recorded and where you can get information from.

Finally, get your hands on the other school policies. If your school has a behaviour policy or a calculation policy, you'll need to use them and follow them. It is hard to do that if you haven't read them. The same goes for the school's marking/ feedback policy.

4.   **Have day one planned and resourced.**

Don't leave anything to chance! Get everything done, printed and ready beforehand. If you don't, you are just asking for the printer to stop working or for some other disaster to happen! Those devices of the underworld rarely need more than the slightest excuse to stop working as it is!

Plans will probably change, but if you have the day ready, you'll have more time to adapt to these changes. You'll also sleep way better the night before, safe in the knowledge that you are prepared and ready.

5. **Decide on your classroom rules.**

In general, a lot of this will come from the school's policy. You do however, need to create a system. Will pupils have water at their desk or in an area? Will they be sent for coats a table at a time or in a mass melee?

I'd advise going through the day mentally. What do the pupils do at each point and how do they interact with you, other adults, and their peers? You will need to make this explicit early on to avoid confusion. As mentioned before, pupils like rules and routine. They hate chaos and so you need to be on top of everything from the start.

I'd also recommend having your reward systems in place and ready to share with pupils. I like to have two systems which run parallel to each other: Golden Tickets and Table Points.

The idea behind Golden Tickets is that individual achievements and efforts can be rewarded. The pupil will put their ticket in the box and at the end of the week, I draw five tickets. The winners each get a prize and are congratulated. The class themselves decide to compete between whether boys or girls will draw the most tickets each week. The girls tend to win but that is by design; I have a lot of shy girls compared to loud, over-confident boys. I'm going to let you in on a little secret and I sincerely hope none of my former pupils ever read this part: the draw is a fix! I glance in the box first, grab the ticket I want draw, then mix my hand around the box to give the illusion that I'm shuffling them. The pupils haven't caught on yet. Sometimes it isn't needed but on other occasions, you know that so-and-so just needs a boost or so-and-so-mark-two have tried so hard and this could validate that effort a little bit more.

I should note here that there is a lot of theory to suggest that a prize-based reward system isn't a good idea. I find the theory really interesting but as I am yet to find a practical replacement that works with my class, I am currently sticking to what seems to work.

My second reward system focuses more on a peer-pressure basis. Each table is given a name and I may award points for good learning behaviours shown table-wide. This has an impact as subconsciously, pupils don't want to let each other down. Some will try harder to earn table points for the sake of their peers, than they will to earn individual rewards.

I would recommend however, that this doesn't become an excuse for pupils to be unkind to others. If that is the case, you may need to change this system. In recent months, I have dropped this as I found that some pupils were becoming stressed at the competition and the thought of their peers blaming them. Now, we try to tidy up quickly, but the focus is on tidying because we understand the value of having a neat, organised classroom, as opposed to prizes. The pupils tidy because they want to look neat and smart for anyone who visits the room.

6.   **Get to know other staff.**

Ensure that you meet your Teaching Assistant (TA) and any other relevant adults before starting. They will be able to guide you throughout your career and are invaluable parts of your class's teaching team. Yes, you are a team – don't worry, it doesn't all fall on you!

I was quite lucky to be honest. My TA worked really hard to build a relationship with me early on and even came in during the summer holidays to help me get ready. I'd like to think that I wasn't exactly a pain of a human to work with, though I have to admit, I can be quite quiet in new situations and this can be interpreted as rudeness. Whilst I was lucky, I do think it is worth encouraging you to go the extra-mile to be friendly and show them that you are there to work with them. A lot of teachers come into schools with an attitude that their TA is like a servant and they (the teacher) don't need their TA's help with the teaching side of things. This is sorely untrue, and those teachers will soon sink and sink fast. However, I can imagine that every TA must worry about that sort of teacher being paired with them and as such, you should be clear that you are a team player and keen to take on-board their experience. To be honest, they've probably forgotten more than you or me will ever know!

The school you are in should also run like a well-oiled machine. This can only happen if every part of the machine is in-sync with the others. You will have to liaise with a lot of staff and it is helpful if they have at least heard of you! Go introduce yourself! Be polite! If they have a dog, coo over pictures of it! That's how to get me to like you anyway...

To offer you one final piece of advice: Be confident. You may not be of course. In fact, you'll probably be bricking it! I was! Let me re-phrase this: Act confident. That's much better!

You see, you'll soon be meeting your new pupils, staff-team, and parents/carers for the first time. Your interactions should be on your terms to help people realise that you know what you're doing and that you are engaged with your job.

Be proactive; meet and greet pupils and parents at the gate/ door of the classroom. Introduce yourself, shake hands and make eye-contact - let the parents know that you are open to talk if they want to discuss anything with you. Get them onside early. If you stand in corner shyly, you give the impression that you are lost, and this will just make things slightly harder for you – especially if you are young-looking.

Chapter 3 – Parents

It may seem unusual that this chapter is placed so early given that it is an area of teaching in which your control is limited. I place it early however, as I remember how much the other NQTS around me wanted some training on this. I was a bit unsure myself really.

Through teacher-training, you take over a wide-range of aspects relating to teaching and the classroom. However, it is quite unusual for a trainee to ever fully take over communications with a pupil's home. At the end of the day, the buck stops with the class teacher and the parents know this. They aren't really interested in you and the class teacher knows this, and so they have to keep on top of it themselves. On the other hand, without needing to take over this aspect of daily life, you are free to focus on teaching and developing your own practice which let's face it, is what you're meant to be doing.

Now, you're the class teacher. You're the one in the cross-hairs. Gulp! If you're feeling a knot forming in your stomach right now, don't worry. I've made this out to be scarier than it is. In general, parents are fine and the (rare) ones that aren't, would probably be that way with anybody – don't take it personally. I will however, detail some easy-to-use methods that will help you to establish a good parent-teacher relationship early on.

Or at least, I will once my dog stops pawing my leg for love and attention. I thought one hand fussing her was enough while I typed. Apparently not...

Get Parents On-side

I won't go into a whole bit about why engaging parents is important – we know it already. We know how important they are to a child's life and we know that they want the best for their children. We should want to build a good relationship with parents and it is actually surprisingly easy to do so. I can hear you asking me now, what makes it so easy?

Principle One (see chapter one) – simple. Parents and teachers are both governed by that same principle: put the kids first. Even if you have a disagreement with them, how can any reasonable parent ever have a huge problem with you, when you're putting their child above everything. Parents are wired to love you for that! You may disagree with each other of course, but by making it clear that you are thinking of their child first, any discussions will be far more constructive. You will need to show this in your actions too (on a day-to-day basis) and make it clear in any meetings you have with parents. It won't work if you do nothing but bemoan their child or don't celebrate any of their successes. In many meetings, I'd even point out how much you like their child, just to be clear. This is true of course, and so it will come across as genuine. You and the parents may disagree on the method, but you're on the same side!

That's the theory of course but I promised way back in the introduction that I would focus solely on providing practical advice. The first piece I will offer is probably the most important one: make a positive connection. If you have made a positive connection, when you need to discuss something less positive, it won't seem like you are a negative person who only sees the worse in their little sweety-pie.

Here are some tips to help you build this relationship:

- Always meet parents with a handshake and a "How are you?" at the door. Coo over their baby if they bring a pushchair into school. You could tell them how lovely it looks even if it doesn't (I don't get the whole 'cute' baby thing).

- Make yourself visible and happy-looking when they are around. Stand tall but have a wide, opening stance to appear both confident and approachable. If parents do want to enquire about anything, they should feel able to. If they don't, their concerns may fester and grow into something harder to deal with.

- Talk to them about the good things that have happened. At the end of the school day, go out and say to them, "Hi Mr/Ms So-and-so, I just wanted to catch you to share this brilliant bit of work that So-and-so Junior did today. I'm so proud of him/her (as an involved teacher, you'll probably know the gender of the child, so delete as appropriate)."

If you need to, get on the phone at the end of the day. Ring them up and share the great learning that their child has been doing. It'll have a positive impact on the pupil anyway but will also clearly show them how much you care about their child. Don't let the parents' absence from school discourage you from making a connection. Ring, send postcards, do anything you need to, but share the positives with them!

Managing Conflict

Although quite rare, there will be circumstances where your relationship with

parents won't be all sunshine and lollipops.
Sometimes parents can be rude or irritating or
refuse to listen to anything that contradicts what
their little angel has told them. At these points,
it's important to remain professional and stand
frim in your belief that the child comes first –
this will give you the inspiration you need to
carry on trying to solve whatever issue has
arisen.

Conflict can arise from a range of different
possibilities. In my experience however, the
most common reason for conflict stems from a
lack of communication. A minor incident gets
blown out-of-proportion when communication
is impaired, and half-truths get thrown into the
mix.

Take for example, a playground scuffle. They happen. We deal with and using restorative practice, we aim to resolve the situation and develop the involved pupils' emotional capacity to help them better understand how to manage a similar situation in the future. Let's assume this has happened and that you, as the class teacher, has dealt with it. There are now two ways this can play out with respect to parental communication:

Option One: You decline to tell the parent. I'm not judging as sometimes it is an awkward thing to do, especially when you're new to the profession. You're not hiding anything of course, you've dealt with it and it's done; why do you need to open it back up? That's what you convince yourself anyway. This is where it helps to have a strong relationship with your TA as they can tell you to go and deal with it. My TA can tell a mile away when I'm avoiding something awkward and gives me a look that I can't escape from.

The problem with not going out is that the whole incident can get blown out of proportion whilst you're not there. Maybe one of kids tells their parents and, as kids do, leave out the part where they did X, Y, and Z. Maybe the parent then believes that their child has been attacked and you, the demonic class teacher, had the audacity to punish both of them! This feeling of injustice spirals around in the parent's head all night until by morning, they are convinced that their poor child is the victim of a bullying campaign and that you are not just enabling this to happen, but effectively punishing their child for it! What reasonable parent isn't going to be infuriated?

None of that is the truth of course and you'll be completely caught off guard when the parent comes steaming in the next day, ready to bite your head off and throw your decapitated body to the wolves. You may be able to calm the situation down and explain the truth (often the kids admit to their part at this point and leave their parents looking a bit foolish), but it will likely take longer to do so. Whilst you haven't done anything wrong necessarily, it will probably damage your relationship with that parent as well. They will still feel a bit unhappy and if their child has made them look a fool, they will subconsciously blame you a little as well.

In the worst case, the parent may simply refuse to listen to you, damaging your relationship even more. Your Senior Leadership Team will probably step in at this point or if not, ask them to. There is nothing wrong with saying, *"I understand your concerns Mr/Ms So-and-so, but as I do have to begin my lesson now; would you mind if we schedule a meeting for later in the day to discuss this further and resolve the situation? Don't worry if not, I know you're busy. I could find Mr/Mrs SLT for you to talk for a moment, if that is any better?"*

Your Senior Leadership Team will support you of course. As an NQT, we sometimes worry that we must appear perfect at all times but in some cases, a fresh (and more-experienced) face can often help. SLT are there to help with situations like this and would rather you involved them to help de-escalate something, than you pig-headedly carried on so as not to appear like you can't handle it. Being able to handle something doesn't necessarily mean you should – someone else may be in a better position to get a better result. At the end of the day, you are a team and the members of that team should work together. Note that if you do arrange a meeting for later, ensure that a member of your Senior Leadership Team joins you, just for added support.

I've spent a bit of time explaining what to do in the case that you choose option one as at some point, you may do so – maybe by accident. Let's now look at option two – my recommendation to you.

Option Two: At the end of the school day, you nip out to the parent and let them know what has happened, but also that you've dealt with it. Tell them how you're *"just letting them know"* but that you are on top of it and both pupils have agreed what to do if anything like this happens again.

The parents will appreciate being kept in the loop (which improves your relationship further as they won't subconsciously think you are hiding anything) and it stops the rumour-mill spinning. You have laid out the facts and what has been done to resolve the issue. Done.

As it is the part that most NQTs worry about, I will quickly summarise this mini-section regarding conflict:

- Build strong relationships in the beginning.
- Keep parents informed.
- Stand your ground and be honest.
- Remain professional.
- If you feel uncomfortable with any situation (or feel as if it is getting out of hand), refer it to SLT. They will support you and use their wider experience to handle it better. They won't judge you or be unhappy with you (provided you have acted professionally throughout).
- One thing I didn't mention in detail but that is obvious -admit to mistakes if you've made any. You can then rectify them, and the problem will be sorted. To summarise, don't be pig-headed!

Open Evenings

Also known as parents' evening, your school will host regular open evenings. These are fun evenings where you will stay late at school, get no work done, and have to talk to people (the latter being the worse part for me). Joking aside, open evenings are often a very pleasant night where you will get the chance to share and celebrate your pupils' successes – which let's face it, are our successes too.

Your school will likely provide you with training on how they want you to structure these nights, but for the sake of this book, I will explain how I structure mine following my school's guidance. Just a quick tip: once parents have indicated what time they would like for the night, and once you have made a timetable and given parents a specific time, keep a copy of that timetable for yourself. This probably seems obvious but on my first open evening, I had sent out exact times but made no note of them. I had no idea what order the parents were supposed to be in or when they were coming! I was saved as my teaching assistant (who rescues me on a daily basis) had thankfully kept a note of it all, but the night could have descended into chaos if not.

Firstly, ensure that your classroom (or wherever the parents will be) is tidy and clean. I like to have the room spotless with pupils each piling their books in their place. I even go as far as to insist upon the order with which they stack their exercise books to ensure that they look neat. I'd spray some air-freshener before the start of the night and play some nice, relaxing music. This creates a nice atmosphere and, if you are having to discuss pupils in the corner of the classroom, the music provides a bit of cover to give you (and the parent/guardians) a bit of extra privacy. Finally, I like to run a slideshow of pictures taken throughout the year. It runs on a loop and gives something for the parents to enjoy whilst they wait.

Secondly, have your table set up ready for these meetings. I am lucky enough to have an adjoining room with a huge window to my classroom, and another to the corridor. I have my meetings in there for the privacy the room provides. This works well as I can see parents in the classroom and can go and get them when it is their turn. Also, your headteacher will probably be roaming throughout the night to check if anyone needs support. He or she (in my case, she) can look in easily and see that everything is OK. Also, not that it has happened, but she would be able to see and step in if something wasn't. From her perspective, she wants to show her face and continue to build on some of the relationships she has built with parents too.

I would also ensure that you have all your information with you. I bring my Purple Book (mentioned earlier) so that I can quickly and easily access information such as homework completion, attendance, and spelling test scores. If I still need a letter signed, I can also notice that and ask them to fill it in there and then. If you don't have information on a pupil's attendance, I would recommend asking the staff in the office to print it out for you. If there happen to be any attendance problems, this is a good time to discuss them.

As simple as it sounds, I also bring a notebook and pen with me. The odds are that a few parents will either have concerns or mention something that you need to follow up. I like to be open about writing these down so that parents can see that I've made a note about their concern and will definitely address it, not just forget. I explain to them that I'm making a note to remind me to follow it up, of course. I don't just sit writing secretive notes whilst in the discussion – I don't want to make anyone paranoid!

As a final touch in your preparations, consider having some refreshments either in the room or wherever you intend to talk to the parents. Sometimes (and certainly in my current school), this is already taken care of and so you won't have to do anything.

After all of the above has been completed, it will be time for the night to start. My headteacher is very keen on making these evenings more of a discussion than just teacher and parent talking at one another. As such, she encourages the class teaching assistants to stay and support in conversations (giving them time-back at a later date). This has been a life-saver to me as my current teaching assistant is very experienced, passionate, and good at helping me get out of holes! If this isn't practice at your school, I'd recommend suggesting it to your Senior Leadership Team – bonus points for your innovation!

I tend to start each meeting by greeting the parents warmly, shaking their hands and inviting them in. I think this is a professional way to start such meetings and sets a good example for any pupils nearby. Silly as it may sound, these moments may stick in a child's mind for years and help them later when meeting someone professionally or when going to a job interview.

I've read countless articles detailing long-winded ways to start meetings which aim to give you a psychological edge over the other person, but I have to admit; I don't do them. I'm not going to war with these parents; we're going to be having a nice discussion. Why play games? I'd recommend that you cut through that sort of rubbish; you're a teacher, not a multimillion-pound businessperson negotiating a deal worth more than you'll ever earn. Relax.

If the child in question is in the meeting, I might start by asking them how they think the year has gone go so far. If not – or if they sit frozen as they will tend to do for some reason – I will then begin with the positives. I like to discuss what subjects the pupil is doing well in before I discuss any areas in which they need to improve. I then like to end with something else positive about the child that I have noticed. I feel that this helps to create a more positive environment and really, that is what you want an open evening to be like.

Also, ensure that you do have a plan of what you want to discuss as awkward silences can be uncomfortable. I then tend to finish off by asking if the parents have anything they'd like to discuss or ask. At the end, shake hands again and wish them the best.

If you're unsure what to discuss, try to follow this checklist:

- Something positive about their academic performance,
- Something you'd like them to work on,
- Something else positive about them,
- Homework and spellings (have they been done to a high-standard?),
- The child's social situation (parents like to know that their child has friends and is happy),
- Time for the parents to discuss their thoughts or concerns.

Hopefully this chapter has given you an overview of how to build a strong relationship with the parents and carers of the pupils in your class. They really aren't anything to be worried about, especially for passionate, dedicated teachers like you and me. In fact, I can't recall any incidents I've had with parents so far in these meetings.

Chapter 4 – Behaviour Management (Low-Level Disruption)

In my opinion, managing behaviour is one of the greatest challenges facing any Newly Qualified Teacher – especially if you're working at a new school. It's hard because you are expected to keep 'control' of your class whilst simultaneously using all of the positive strategies you have learnt about throughout your training. What I mean by this, is that there is a misconception that a teacher cannot be firm without seeming mean or out of control. This isn't actually true, being firm is a necessary part of good behaviour management and people aren't judging you or criticising you for it.

I have split the overall area of 'Behaviour Management' into two chapters as I see the skill as being split into two categories: handling low-level disruption and dealing with more challenging issues. This chapter will focus on the former, given how important it is to establish a secure, productive learning-environment.

Setting out your Expectations

It is absolutely imperative that you are clear about your expectations for behaviour, not just in your own mind but when communicating with the children. When I say communicating, I don't just mean verbally either – your visual cues and body language also give away a lot about the standards you have in your classroom.

In the past, you have likely trained with a teacher who has already decided how they like their classroom to run. They will have set out their expectations early on and then later, you will have received the benefits when you came to them on your placement. If, like me, you trained on a one-year school-based teaching course, you will have probably seen your mentor set out their expectations at the start of the year. However, also like me, you may have completely missed the subtleties of how they did this.

In this guide, I aim to skip the theory (on the basis that you have already sat through hours upon hours of boring PowerPoint slides that have given you this knowledge) to give you more practical advice. In this case however, I think it is important to briefly recap why expectations are key. Children need rules. They crave them as rules and boundaries mean that they are safe and know what is expected of them. There is no guess work involved. I mentioned an example earlier which detailed how a pupil can relax in the knowledge that people aren't allowed to hit one another. It seems daft, but it shouldn't be assumed that pupils know these basic rules. If it were not specified, the pupil in question may feel uneasy each time someone walked past them.

Consider another example in which it isn't specified that pupils shouldn't talk over one another. Perhaps in their home setting, they have learnt that the only way to be heard is to talk (or shout) the loudest. Imagine then, their frustration when they have a good idea, share it over the top of another pupil (or teacher), and are then criticised for shouting out. Who said you had to wait your turn? These may seem like minor things but to the pupil, it could give them a negative memory of school about the teacher who just didn't care about their idea. That isn't the case of course, the teacher is just wanting the child to take their turn. To the child however, as they can't see anything wrong with shouting out, they have been silenced for no reason. On the other side, from your perspective, one child shouting out can disrupt the flow and pace of your lesson. Imagine thirty of them doing it – I've been there!

The best piece of advice I can give to you on this subject is a piece that I mentioned earlier in the chapter relating to starting the year well. Decide on your expectations, take some lesson time to share these clearly (getting your pupils' opinions too as you want them to agree with the rules) and then stick to them rigidly. It will be even better if you can manipulate the lesson so that the pupils think they are deciding on these rules themselves.

If you want pupils to raise their hands, don't accept answers from pupils shouting out (I'm bad at this one). If you want a straight line at the end of breaktime, then wait for a straight line at the end of breaktime (they can always pay back the time they are wasting through their next break). If you expect pupils to work in silence for a task, then don't allow them to not be silent. Especially at the start of the year, you need to be firm and unwavering with your expectations. This will pay dividends in the long run!

Your Personality

Pupils will take a lead from you and copy everything you do. Whether you like it or not, you will quickly become a role-model for the thirty-plus children in your class. If you are a snappy, miserable person, the pupils will become irritable with each other and copy your rude behaviours. I've seen occasions in which members of staff treat children like dirt (not deliberately but as a way of trying to be firm) and then become outraged when a child responds in kind. I'm not defending the child being rude to an adult, but they learnt the behaviour from somewhere. Children are like sponges and, even if it isn't done consciously, they pick up and learn their social skills from us – they spend enough time with us to do so!

This trait, of course, plays right into your hands. If you model the behaviour you expect from children, then overall, they will copy it. If you are kind and thoughtful, your pupils will become more considerate to each other. If you are calm and don't rush to judgement, the pupils will be calmer in situations in which they are unhappy. They will be far more open to a calm discussion, if they see you calmly discuss things with successful outcomes.

Two of the best teachers I have ever seen were experts in this field. I was fortunate enough to spend time with them both throughout my training year and the way in which they handled difficult classes was nothing short of amazing. In the whole school year, not once did either of them raise their voice or ever seem out of control. I try my best to emulate their style of behaviour management and am getting better, although it is harder than it looks to be entirely honest. So, how do they do it?

(I) Firstly, both of them have a very calm, confident air about them when teaching. When the pupils are out of the way, they are different, normal people, but in the classroom, they maintain this persona. Neither will shout or raise their voice – it isn't necessary. In fact, such things will likely escalate any potential problems that are forming. Instead, they talk at a reasonable volume and pace, and wait for pupils to be listening. This atmosphere creates a relaxed environment where pupils don't need to worry about getting told off or making mistakes with respect to behaviour.

Contrast this to a teacher who snaps at anybody who is not doing what they want. This teacher will create a fear factor in the classroom and cause pupils to be scared of making mistakes. I don't know about you, but I'd rather have a child who misses an instruction because their mind has wandered deeper into something challenging about their last bit of learning, than one who is too scared to think about anything other than what instructions are being barked at them.

(II) This brings me to a second tip for you, waiting, praising, and re-iterating. One of the biggest disruptions throughout lessons are the moments when children are in transition. They might be coming into the classroom, getting their books, or even just putting their equipment down to listen to the next part of your lesson. I see countless teachers handle this is in a natural, but out-dated, way. See the example below:

Teacher: Right class, put your things down and look at me. Come on, quickly now. Alice, I'm waiting for you to put your pen down and listen. Ben, Charlie, no one asked you to be out of your seats – sit down. Oak Table, do I have to keep you in at break-time or are you going to hurry up? I've told you once, Alice! Put. The. Pen. Down.

Right, we're ready. So, on the board... Alice! Look this way!

I'm confident that we've all had a moment like this, whether we like to admit it or not. There are positives from this by the way, I'm not going to just criticise the hypothetical teacher above. In fact, a big plus is that the teacher clearly has a standard which he/she requires to be met. The pupils should put their equipment down and face the board. He/she is sticking to their standard, not just trying to talk over the class and hope someone is listening (silly as it sounds, I see that a lot too!)

This teacher has the right idea! Have a standard and stick to it. It is his/her execution of this that is less than perfect. It is quite negative overall and the pupils who aren't yet following the instructions, are named-and-shamed in front their peer-group. Alternatively, have a look at the example below:

Teacher: Ok then everybody. I'm going to countdown from 5 and then I'm looking for everybody to be facing the front with their pens on the table.

5

4

Oooo! Well done Dan, who has put his pen down and is looking at me. Well done Alice, who is about to put her pen down. Good job!

3

2

Well done Maple Table. All of that table is ready. The same with Berch Table. And now a few others, well done.

1

0

Brilliant. Well done those people who are ready to carry on learning. I'm just waiting for 2 people now. Just 1. There we go, everyone is ready.

This time, the teacher has followed the waiting, praising, and re-iterating idea. He/she has given a set of clear instructions and has given a timeline with which pupils can complete this. It is unrealistic to expect a pupil to be really engaged with their writing, but then simultaneously expect them to drop their pen instantly, mid-sentence, just because you want to talk. By giving them a countdown, they can choose an appropriate stopping point.

Further to this, pupils who have completed the instructions aren't just ignored – they are rewarded. These pupils have a tendency to lose out on attention as it is assumed that they will choose to follow instructions everytime. In this example however, they get the positive attention of praise and as a side note, other pupils notice this and want to get some themselves. Don't forget, pupils love attention! Note how Alice was still named but in a positive way. In the first example, Alice was criticised a lot. In the second example, she is praised for being about to do something. In all likelihood, she is now more inclined to do so because she has had the instructions re-iterated to her in a more friendly, positive way. If not, I might catch her eye to focus her back on the instructions. This doesn't draw any negative attention to her but reminds her that I am prepared to wait for her focus.

Throughout the countdown, the instructions are re-iterated multiple times. This way, pupils who didn't hear or who have forgotten (some pupils will genuinely struggle to remember everything) can still 'achieve' so to speak. They can complete the task and be praised for that.

In my experience, pupils are generally ready by the time I get to zero. If not, I tend to simply wait and show that I'm waiting. I still don't need to name-and-shame and the peer pressure of being the only ones not ready will help convince the other children to follow the instructions. The class is then focused on the next part of lesson, without any negativity being released into the room.

(III) Thirdly, if a pupil is continually disruptive, ask yourself why? It may be linked to a larger issue (in which case, the next chapter may be more appropriate). In my experience, if it isn't linked to something bigger, it is to do with the task that the pupil in question is trying to complete.

This can go two ways: too easy, or too hard. I tend to think that each pupil has a 'Goldilocks

Region' which the task should fall into, preferably closer to the 'Too Hard' region to provide more challenge. If the work set however, falls outside of this imaginary region, the pupils will be unable to access it (or disengaged if it isn't challenging enough) and will seek entertainment elsewhere. It may be that they become distracted and start to talk. It may be that they happen to need the toilet and then, when they haven't produced a lot of work, it is because they went there and not because they couldn't do it (pupils hate to feel like failures).

It is important that pupils are given work that they can access and that they can succeed with. In most cases, this will fall within your standard differentiation although for some pupils it may require more thought. Let's look first at a pupil who is finding the work too challenging. They may be behind their classmates and if so, they probably know it. They may have an attitude that they are stupid or can only do work if an adult sits with them. Maybe they disrupt to hide from this work, maybe it is just because they're bored as they can't do it. There is also the possibility that they are jealous of their peers. These pupils get so much attention for doing well. By acting up or disrupting they will get some sort attention, even if it isn't positive.

A quick way to reduce the disruption this child causes is to remember that they are not different to any other pupil – they want to achieve and for people (including yourself) to be proud of them. By giving them appropriate tasks and praising them, we encourage them to work hard and feel the same sense of success that everyone strives for. Just a quick note by the way: adult support is not the same as giving a pupil a differentiated task! There is a time for it, but it will rarely build confidence or independence. I'd far prefer to give such a pupil an appropriate, independent task and keep checking in with them. That way, they are learning to work and achieve successes independently, but I am still keeping tabs on them and addressing misconceptions. Pupils who work with an adult too much become dependent on them and unless you are prepared to follow them around throughout their adult-life to help them, you are just passing this problem on to the next teacher.

This task doesn't have to relate to the learning objective by the way. Why have the pupil learning how to use relative clauses when they still struggle with a simple sentence? We could use this learning time to strengthen their knowledge on something appropriate to them, and then visit relative clauses with them later on, when the lesson will be better received. You don't want to put a ceiling on a child's learning, but they also need to learn how to walk before they can run.

Another way to support these pupils is through a pre-teach. I found pre-teaches annoyingly useless when I first started my NQT year but over time, I learnt how to use them effectively and now, I'm all for them! The idea is that they are there to help the pupils access the learning for the lesson. Initially, I thought they were just another type of meaningless intervention. A classic 'SLT said to do intervention in the morning so we are doing intervention in the morning whether it is beneficial or not' kind of thing – we all know what I mean. Instead, the pre-teach should relate to your next lesson. You, or another adult, supports these pupils in the method and key words so that the pupils can not only access the learning in the lesson on an independent basis, but that they can contribute to the classroom discussion and main input. What a confidence boost for them!

On the flip-side of your differentiation, pupils may also be finding the work too easy. In a way, this is harder to deal with as challenges require more thought. They need to be at a level which stretches the pupil, but not so difficult that they discourage them from trying new things. I feel that the best way to deal with this sort of pupil is to work hard to create a mindset with them where they learn to enjoy challenges. That way, the pupil can be stretched without moving from the 'Too Easy' zone, straight to the 'Too Hard' zone.

You won't get this right straight away of course, it's impossible. However, over time you will get to know each of your pupils and will be able to plan better, more appropriate lessons.

PIP and RIP

This whole concept has really stuck a chord with me and it is so useful that I'd highly recommend you use it as well.

PIP stands for Praise in Public. Basically, when a pupil does something good or displays positive learning behaviours, make sure that everyone knows about it. Not only are you aiming to praise them for this behaviour, but you want to provide them with the attention they crave. In addition, their peers will also notice the good learning and seek to emulate it themselves. This whole concept creates a positive cycle in your classroom.

However, there is the still the question what can be done when pupils demonstrate negative behaviour despite your range of positive strategies. This is where RIP comes in: Reprimand in Private. That is, discuss the negative behaviour (and a way forward) with the child away from their peers. People are proud and although we think of school as a learning establishment, to children, it is a social jungle. By shouting at them or calling them out in front of their peers, we challenge their self-worth and trigger the child's fight or flight instinct. They will either fight (shout at you or escalate the issue) or run (hide from the problem and not listen to your advice on how to avoid it in the future).

By quietly talking to the pupil in private, we can have a better conversation, with more productive outcomes. We protect their ego and we don't risk a battle in the middle of a lesson which frankly, just wastes useful learning time. In addition, we don't give out our attention to negative behaviour – at least, not in front of the class. This maintains the status quo that the best way to be acknowledged and receive adult attention is to do something positive.

You may be asking then, what to do when a pupil is disrupting the class and not responding to strategies already discussed, such as praising the pupils on task. I tend to re-iterate the instruction to give them another chance but, if they don't comply and if I can do so, I'll simply ignore it. I'm not prepared to waste the learning time of other pupils to give my attention to this pupil without good reason. In effect, I starve the fire of the oxygen it needs to continue or grow. If pupils are becoming distracted, just re-iterate what they should be doing and praise them again for their attention.

In small cases, like Alice day-dreaming, you can quietly squat down next to her table (during the next activity) and mention how you'd like her to make sure she is paying attention. This is more effective that shouting for her to pay attention mid-input.

Word of Advice

As a final part to this chapter, I have to say: don't expect too much of yourself. It is really hard to manage the low-level stuff in a classroom and a lot comes with practice and experience. You will not be able to walk into a room and magically make every student in the class turn into a polite, keen, learning machine. You can do your best. You can keep learning. This is a hard part of teaching that you shouldn't expect to master straight away.

I do hope however, that some of the tips in this section will help you.

Chapter 5 – Behaviour Management (Difficult Cases)

Sometimes, either because something went wrong with how a low-level incident was dealt with or because of events out of your control, you will face a child who may be in crisis point. Crisis point is the point a child reaches where they just can't listen to reason anymore. They may be angry, upset or any range of emotions, but these emotions are extreme and to the child, nothing else in the world matters more in that moment.

We all have a tipping point albeit different for everybody. For teachers like ourselves, that point is almost impossible to get to as it wouldn't be appropriate for us to lose our temper in school. We take this for granted although actually, we developed our ability to manage our emotions in the same way we learnt any other skill we have. The skill of emotional control is learnt through our interactions from birth and it stays with us. For example, when something is wrong, we learn as a baby that if we cry and make loud noises, someone will come and fix it. This explains why in later life, we may cry when we secretly want someone to just come and fix whatever has upset us – even if that's unlikely to happen.

We also learn other things about our emotional limits and how they comply with social norms. Growing up, we all have a moment when another child has a toy and we want it. At some point, we will take the toy and then get told off (and hopefully have it explained that it upsets the other child). We learn that sometimes we need to control our wants as stealing is wrong (or at the very least, we may be punished). Early on in life, we tend to learn a key principle that we should treat other people in the same way in which we would like to be treated.

For some of our children, they have not developed these skills as fast as their peers. This can happen for a range of reasons and as teachers, we should aim to support their development. Of course, this lack of development isn't always recognised, and these pupils become labelled as 'bad'.

This brings us to the second point we should consider when a child is in crisis point. Not only is the child unable to calmly evaluate their emotions, they also have many years of experience behind them telling them that they are a bad person, and that adults think of them as bad. Why would you listen and open up to somebody who just thinks you're a bad person anyway? This lack of trust can amplify problems further and further, creating a sense of isolation for the child.

I could go on and on about this and provide a book dedicated solely to it; as you can probably tell, this is one parts of teaching I am quite passionate about. However, I will limit myself to some practical ideas which you may be able to use in your setting. Your school - and SENCO in particular - will be able to provide you with more support with these pupils anyway and you should make good use of these resources.

Building Trust

As I mentioned above, if a child doesn't trust the adults then why listen to them at all? You need to (and should anyway) be building trust with the pupils in your class from the very start of the year. They need to know early on that you care about each and every one of them, and you need to show them this. If you smile at them, praise them, and take an interest in their lives, they will bond with you and be likely to trust you later.

Meet the pupils at the door and say hello. Ask them how their night was. If they have a picture or a story, give them attention for it in the same way a good parent would. You are a huge part of these pupils' lives and they deserve your love and attention. As a side benefit to this, they will be more likely to respond to you if -or when - they reach their crisis point.

As a final point on this subsection about building trust, I have to strongly recommend that you are always honest with pupils. If you go back on your word, they won't trust you the next time. As an adult, we know that sometimes things happen outside of our control and for that reason, be careful before promising anything. It may seem small but if you promise something, the child will expect you to deliver and if you don't, they will be far more suspicious about the next time you say something. To avoid getting caught in this trap, I don't tend to promise pupils anything other than that I will listen to them fairly, when they are prepared to calm down and discuss the situation in an adult way. This is a promise I can always fulfil as I always have time to listen to them. It also requires something from them – it's a kind of deal. They have a choice: carry on or stop and calmly discuss things. Note that giving pupils a choice like this (no matter how obvious the right answer is) can be a really effective way of helping them to calm down. By making the choice, they start to feel like they have some control over things which relaxes their fight or flight instinct.

At Crisis Point

This is probably the bit that will be useful to you as a front-line class teacher. A child is at crisis point. Whether this is for a valid reason or something frustratingly minor and silly, the reason is big to them and they can't see past it. What do you do? Unfortunately, it isn't easy to say. There are countless ways to handle the situation and the right one is known only by the person who knows the child best – if even they know! I'll try to give you some general ideas though that tend to hold true for most situations that I've encountered.

Firstly, remain calm. It is such a simple thing, but it has such a big impact. If you respond to the situation calmly, it can't escalate. The child will also start to mirror your behaviour and calm themselves down more. If the child is at a point where talking to them may be helpful, speak calmly and clearly to them, regardless of what else is happening. Crouch to their level if possible (so that you aren't looming over them) and look at them when you are talking. Don't discuss the incident - a disagreement will continue the crisis and send the pupil back into their spiral of negativity. Instead, you should give them simple instructions that will help move them to a calm mental space. Have a look at the examples below which could be used to begin to calm a situation down:

"I understand that this has upset you and I'm happy to talk to you calmly about it. For now, though, I'd like you to sit down and take a few deep breaths."

"Maybe so-and-so did do that. I'm happy to discuss this properly once we are both sat down in the so-and-so room and feeling a bit calmer."

In each example, the teacher acknowledged the child's feelings without committing to their side (or more importantly, against their side). The teacher then gives them instructions to follow in a calm manner and doesn't engage with anything inflammatory. The instructions are not controversial, and the child will understand that you are trying to help them to calm down. Even if it takes a while, by repeating the instructions calmly, the child will eventually get themselves to a point where they are ready to comply and move the conversation forward.

I'd recommend that you find a quiet space for the child to go to whilst they calm down. After all, trying to calm down from crisis point isn't easy when the entire class is sat staring at you. Some pupils may have their own safe space in school and giving them some time in it can help them to begin to self-regulate their emotions again.

Once the child has calmed down, you can discuss the issue more clearly. They will be more likely to understand the other points of view and, in private, you will be able to reach a much more constructive conclusion. If the child begins to get upset again, you'll need to be patient and return to whatever you were doing to help them calm down.

It is also important at crisis point that the child doesn't feel backed into a corner. Being surrounded by adults, shouted at, told what to do, or told off are big mistakes that are made commonly. Give them some space - they aren't thinking clearly enough to process what is happening and surrounding them won't help. They are in fight or flight mode and you need to bring them out of it, before discussing other things. This means, you need to simplify their environment to the point that they can start to make heads or tails of what is happening and how they feel. More stimuli, be it people, voices or commands, only adds to the confusion which in turn causes more panic, and then the child keeps spiralling.

If they run away, have someone follow them but not engage in conversation. They may just need space. As long as they aren't trying to leave school grounds or hurt themselves, you can usually afford to give them this space. As a general rule, unless the pupil is doing something dangerous, it may help to simply give them the space they need to let this crisis feeling pass. Of course, if they are a danger to themselves or others, you will need to interfere based on your school policy and statutory duty of care.

Conclusion

To conclude this section, remember that there are no bad kids. You, as the adult, are responsible for finding the most constructive way forward. This means you need to calm situations using a range of methods; do not try to escalate them. If they are in the wrong, you can discuss it later - when they are calm – as part of your good restorative practice.

If these situations happen a lot, perhaps sitting down with the school SENCO will help. The two of you can form a support plan to meet that child's needs and support their behaviour management.

As a final note, situations like these may be evidence of an issue relating to child protection. Report them to your school's safeguarding lead who will make a note of it. It may be another piece in the jigsaw – even if it seems small.

Chapter 6 – Working with Support Staff

This is one of the areas which I remember being a concern amongst my cohort's NQTs. It is quite scary after all. You will very likely be working with someone with more experience than you will ever have – all whilst you're learning yourself. In actual fact, this is possibly the easiest part of teaching. Ninety-nine times out of a hundred, support staff will go out of their way to help you – particularly once you have shown yourself to be a caring staff member. Like you, support staff want the best for the children and are keen to team up with you for their sake.

I was very lucky starting my NQT year in that my TA was (and is) the go-to person when a problem arises. She has so much experience and drive in her job that she can handle anything. In addition, she cares for the pupils and their well-being as much as I do – we were always going to make a good team.

That is, by the way, a key part of working with support staff. You are a team. Some teachers seem to have this idea that they are the team on their own and the TAs or other support staff are their property, like a whiteboard or a metre stick. It seems a strange concept to me and yet, there are those who act in this weird way. If you really want to make a positive difference to the pupils, then you need to work with your TA and listen to them. They have more experience than you and also have the added benefit of seeing more of the lesson. They can pick up on things that you miss whilst doing inputs or other such things.

To be honest, there isn't really much more to say on this whole point. As long as you show everybody the same respect that they are due, you will always get on well with everyone. Just don't fall into the trap of thinking you know better and don't need help or advice. Although if you were likely to do so, you probably wouldn't have made it this far into a book designed to provide you with tips and support.

It really isn't an area that you need to worry about. TAs won't eat you and they are in the class for the same reason you are – the kids. If you do meet that rare one-in-a-hundred who isn't there to help the children, you could always discuss with your mentor how to build bridges with them. There will be a way.

As a final point, remember that TAs aren't psychic. They may be very experienced and know what they're doing, but they didn't plan the lesson. Let them know in advance what you'd like the children to achieve and discuss with them how the two of you should deploy yourselves. I tend to not plan that aspect to be honest. I find that when we discuss it in the morning we create some far better ideas anyway. Plus, you may change it mid-lesson anyway, depending on how you can maximise the learning in the classroom.

Chapter 7 – High Quality Teaching

It would seem strange in a book about teaching not to include some actual tips on how to teach. To be truthful, you tend to learn a lot more in this profession by trying things and reflecting on their success. By reflecting of course, I don't mean filling out endless forms for evidence files, but actually thinking about it yourself. Your TA can provide some good feedback too, they are in the lesson with you after all. As long as you are constantly looking to improve, you're teaching will become better and better. Hopefully, this will also lead to a significant rise in the quality of learning taking place too.

In this chapter, I will share with you some of the things that I think have had the most impact on the learning in my classroom this year. I must admit, I feel a bit nervous about sharing some of my ideas. Writing this book seemed like a good idea at the time, but now I realise it is like laying your teaching soul open to the world. It's terrifying! Do me a favour: go get something nice to eat and drink as you read this chapter, so you won't judge me too harshly!

Live Feedback

I'm a big believer that effective feedback is key to any successful lesson. Pupils need good feedback in any subject from maths, to art, to snowboarding, to anything. It doesn't matter if you are a beginner or a master, a child, or an adult. Feedback is absolutely key. Any pupil needs to know what they are doing right, what they need to improve on, and how to improve. I also believe that this feedback is more effective if it is done at the point of learning, where the learning itself is fresh in the pupil's brain.

There are a range of ways to do this. The obvious one is for you and your TA to patrol the classroom and provide this feedback to pupils. This is quite effective as it means that the two of you can provide top-quality feedback to pupils in the lesson. It does have its downfalls though. If you can't get around to every pupil, you can't give them all that high-quality feedback. It also means that you might inadvertently miss out on giving feedback to the quieter pupils as you struggle with the melee of trying to get around the classroom as quickly as you can. It's also possible that you could lose sight of your lesson as you're too focused on getting to every child.

Whilst this is undoubtedly a good way to provide feedback, you need other ways to do so too. This is one of the reasons why I am a big advocate of sitting pupils in mixed ability groups. The idea behind this is that every pupil has somebody with them who can provide them with feedback, or that they can provide feedback to.

The pupil who has less ability on the task in hand can receive help from their 'coach' who sits next to them. Alongside adult feedback, they have the support of their peer who can provide more immediate help (and will probably enjoy doing so). Pupils can sometimes explain concepts to their peers in ways that we as adults, can't even begin to think of. In turn, the other pupil must consider the subject more deeply to explain it. This develops their own knowledge and helps them to build the skill of peer-assessment, which translates itself to the skill of good self-assessment. In the long-term, this will benefit the pupil further.

I should note here that these pairings are carefully considered. The pairs are not high to low ability. Say you were to rank each pupil from one to thirty on ability, you would sit them as follows:

1:16

2:17

3:18

4:19

...

14:29

15:30

This means that pupils are not overly unbalanced in terms of academic strengths. I would then jiggle this about so that personalities blend a bit better and each pair becomes quite productive. The stigma of the 'Bottom Table' is also lost which in turn, can further help to boost a pupil's confidence.

Another way to provide quick feedback, is to provide pupils with answers at appropriate points (probably only in KS2). Consider a maths lessons where pupils are learning to complete short column multiplication using a written formal method. You may have done an appropriate starter and gone through the method in the input. You may have done some good questioning and used some formative assessment strategies to identify a focus group. The pupils then begin the activity while you and the class TA go about, providing feedback or taking focus groups.

Imagine a class however, when the first few answers have been given to pupils. This can be quite powerful as it means that pupils can attempt a question, check their answer, and see whether they are right or wrong. If they have gotten the answer right, they are developing confidence in their understanding of the method. If not, they can check their method again to see if it was a minor mistake. If they are still wrong, they know to seek extra help from an adult in the room or from their peers. This takes a bit of training as pupils need to know that the answer isn't there for them to copy – it's to give them feedback. In my experience however, it works very well and lets pupils move themselves onto challenges – or seek more support – with more accuracy.

Quick Bursts

Another aspect of my teaching that I really found to have a huge impact on learning is organising the lesson inputs and activities into short, quick bursts. This works well for several reasons which I will detail below.

Firstly, by doing lessons in quick, progressively harder bursts, pupils can develop their skills in reasonable steps. In contrast, I have seen many lessons where pupils are shown a complicated skill and expected to spend the lesson practicing it until they remember it. By building it up slowly, all pupils have the chance to succeed rather than those with the best memories. Challenge can still be provided to pupils as each step will have an element of greater depth or mastery. If anything, they are challenged more as they go into more depth in each aspect.

Secondly, this method of lesson lends itself to some good feedback. I tend to stop after each mini-task (particularly in maths) and quickly run through the answers, allowing for all pupils to see whether they were right or not. Usually, I should have gotten around to supporting them anyway, but just in case, they can see for themselves. If they haven't understood the activity (which they may not have noticed until they saw that they had a few wrong), they can alert me or my TA in lesson. As a precaution, during the next input, the class TA will look quickly in books anyway to determine if any pupils need more support. This makes it unlikely that any pupils who are struggling, slip through the net and don't make progress.

There are other benefits to this, but I thought I'd share the idea rather the long-winded theory. In short, not every lesson needs to be in the starter-main-plenary mould. Change it to whatever you feel will support learning the best.

Be Positive

The final, major thing that has a huge impact on learning is the attitude of the pupils. Since they emulate you, you can help them with this more than you'd think. We want pupils to be positive and have a positive mindset towards learning and school – particularly in subjects like Mathematics which have a stigma surrounding them. If you are positive about learning and trying new things, then the children will learn to be too.

You can help to build this in your classroom by referencing good learning behaviours constantly. If a pupil demonstrates these behaviours, bring it up and praise them for it. Model them in your life, with things you have found difficult. At school, French was my Achilles heel and I share my experiences of struggling in the lessons with my pupils. After all, it may give them confidence to know that everybody struggles with things.

If they see you use those learning behaviours (or reflect on when you didn't but wish you had), they will start to view them as something real and useful – not just useless school stuff that isn't a part of the outside universe. In part, I'm writing this book so that I can go through the long, laborious process of editing it, before publishing it. I will be able to share my frustrations with the pupils, but I'll be able to say I didn't give up. I was resilient when it was hard. I took a risk to publish it with my name – even though it will doubtlessly be judged (by the way, is now a good time to ask you for a nice rating on Amazon? Nothing too extravagant but you may want to shoe-horn the phrase 'witty and brilliant' in there – wink, wink!) On a serious note, I can't expect my pupils to show resilience, take pride in their work, and take risks, if I'm not prepared to do so myself. Once they see you doing leading by example and using these behaviours, they will start to believe in them as well.

Don't be afraid to let your pupils see you as a human. If anything, it will inspire them. A good leader leads by example; none of that 'Do as I say, not as I do' nonsense that belongs in an old, Victorian classroom. I want the pupils to see my passion for learning and self-development. I want them to see me struggle and still try my best. It's good for them – it sets a good example for them in school and in their wider-life.

Chapter 8 – Time Savers

My final chapter is probably the one you're most interested in. I must admit, before I started I was very scared about the workload facing me as a teacher. There are ways to lessen to this workload but to be honest, it will be tough at the start! Forget a work-life balance for the first few weeks, you are going to have loads to do. That's the same with any professional job though, and it will subside as you find your feet and get settled. You'll be surprised how quickly you can mark and plan good lessons after a while. Plus, as an NQT, you'll have twenty percent of your timetable dedicated to your planning and personal development.

The first tip I have for you relates to marking, and how it is different to feedback. Good feedback helps learning but marking is a ridiculously small aspect of feedback that seems to have a huge stigma attached to it. I'd recommend that you try not to write reams of feedback in pupils' books - it takes you ages and they probably won't even read it. In fact, verbal feedback is far more effective, preferably given at the time of learning. You should focus on providing high-quality feedback and let the improvement in the pupil's book do the talking for you. The evidence of your feedback doesn't need to be a written record of everything you've thought and said. The evidence can be the improvement in the child's learning journey. In fact, it should be that improvement as if you've written reams and there is no improvement, your feedback hasn't been effective at all! Live feedback is better anyway and as an added bonus, it does reduce your marking workload.

Secondly, make the best use of your time. As silly as it sounds, every little job that you save time on, adds up. It may be a case that you find a time where staff go home early and so you do your printing and cutting then. That way, you won't have to wait for the printer or for a guillotine to become free. I tend to not leave work before 5:30pm either; simply to avoid traffic. I will get home at around the same time regardless of whether I leave at 5pm or 5:30pm and so I might as well spend that daily thirty minutes reducing my pile of work, rather than sat in traffic. I really hate traffic.

On the subject of the trip home, you need to try to use it to switch off from work. I tend to put on some music and sing my way home at the top of my voice. Then, I can walk through the door, play with dog for a bit and then relax for the night. I try not to bring too much work home - I'd rather stay late at school and try to separate work from home. It helps me stress less.

In addition, keep yourself flexible. Not every lesson has to have prepared slides and resources. Sometimes, it is more effect to keep your lesson more open anyway with pupils leading the lesson. You don't need to have prepared everything on nice sheets when sometimes, you giving them a question on the board (and going through it together afterwards) can be more effective. In short, do whatever will support learning more, not look nice and fancy to anyone walking into your lesson.

Finally, I'd recommend preparing everything you can through less busy times such as holidays. Some lessons, like topic or art, can be planned in advance and in doing so, you can keep ahead of the workload you will have once the term starts. Whilst you won't want to spend your holidays working too hard, it is much less stressful to plan a few lessons during a day off, than it is to be doing it late at night, worried that you won't be finished in time. By having these lessons planned and resourced, you can relax and focus more on the day-to-day lessons which need to be more responsive.

If you are working in a year group where you have fellow teachers, you may want to work together to share planning for foundation subjects. I've trained in schools who do this, and they tend to make it work quite well. You may however, be like me, in a single-form entry school. In this case, you can't share the workload but everything you plan will save you time next year, at least.

Chapter 9 - Conclusion

I sincerely hope that this small guide has given you some ideas and tips on how to have a successful NQT year. If nothing else, at least you may have learnt from my mistakes.

I won't lie to you – it's a tough year. The first term is also the hardest by far and the one where most people doubt themselves and their career choice. This is the worse scenario because new teachers struggle with the toughest term and with a new job at the same time. That said, you will make it through it and at some point, you will get to the point I'm at, where you love your job. Okay, I still have days where I wonder why I do it, but in all honesty, I wouldn't trade it for anything.

My final words of advice: stick with it! You won't regret it!

Printed in Great Britain
by Amazon